P9-CBR-158

TOOLS FOR CAREGIVERS

- **F&P LEVEL:** C
- **WORD COUNT:** 19

- **CURRICULUM CONNECTIONS:** holidays, traditions

Skills to Teach

- **HIGH-FREQUENCY WORDS:** is, it, we
- **CONTENT WORDS:** candles, dance, decorate, eat, gifts, give, Kwanzaa, light, make, music
- **PUNCTUATION:** exclamation points, periods
- **WORD STUDY:** /k/, spelled c (*candles*, *decorate*, *music*); long /e/, spelled ea (*eat*)
- **TEXT TYPE:** factual description

Before Reading Activities

- Read the title and give a simple statement of the main idea.
- Have students "walk" through the book and talk about what they see in the pictures.
- Introduce new vocabulary by having students predict the first letter and locate the word in the text.
- Discuss any unfamiliar concepts that are in the text.

After Reading Activities

Explain to readers that Kwanzaa celebrates African heritage. Flip back through the book as a group. How are the people in the book celebrating this holiday? Singing and dancing are just two ways. What other ways do readers see?

Tadpole Books are published by Jump!, 5357 Penn Avenue South, Minneapolis, MN 55419, www.jumplibrary.com

Copyright ©2022 Jump! International copyright reserved in all countries. No part of this book may be reproduced in any form without written permission from the publisher.

Editor: Jenna Gleisner **Designer:** Molly Ballanger

Photo Credits: Shutterstock, cover, 14–15; Scott Van Blarcom/Dreamstime, 1; rolf bruderer/Getty, 3; AvailableLight/iStock, 4–5; Inti St. Clair/Getty, 2tl, 2bl, 6–7; DiversityStudio1/Dreamstime, 2br, 8–9; track5/iStock, 2tr, 10–11; Hill Street Studios/Getty, 2ml, 2mr, 12–13; Purestock/Alamy, 16.

Library of Congress Cataloging-in-Publication Data
Names: Zimmerman, Adeline J., author.
Title: Kwanzaa / by Adeline J. Zimmerman.
Description: Minneapolis, Minnesota: Jump!, Inc., (2022) | Series: Holiday fun! | Includes index. | Audience: Ages 3–6
Identifiers: LCCN 2020047838 (print) | LCCN 2020047839 (ebook) | ISBN 9781636900933 (hardcover)
ISBN 9781636900940 (paperback) | ISBN 9781636900957 (ebook)
Subjects: LCSH: Kwanzaa—Juvenile literature.
Classification: LCC GT4403 .Z56 2022 (print) | LCC GT4403 (ebook) | DDC 394.2612—dc23
LC record available at https://lccn.loc.gov/2020047838
LC ebook record available at https://lccn.loc.gov/2020047839

KWANZAA

by Adeline J. Zimmerman

TABLE OF CONTENTS

tadpole
books

WORDS TO KNOW

candles

dance

gifts

give

light

music

KWANZAA

It is Kwanzaa!

kinara ·····▶

We decorate.

We light candles.

drum

We make music.

We dance!

11

gift

We give gifts.

13

We eat.

LET'S REVIEW!

Kwanzaa is a holiday that celebrates African heritage. It starts on December 26. How is this family celebrating?

INDEX